Famous Modern
Negro Musicians

Da Capo Press Music Reprint Series

MUSIC EDITOR
BEA FRIEDLAND
Ph.D., City University of New York

Famous Modern Negro Musicians

BY

PENMAN LOVINGGOOD

With a New Introduction By
EILEEN SOUTHERN

DA CAPO PRESS • NEW YORK • 1978

Library of Congress Cataloging in Publication Data

Lovinggood, Penman.
  Famous modern Negro musicians.

  (Da Capo Press music reprint series)
  Reprint of the 1921 ed. published by Press Forum Co.,
Brooklyn.
  1. Afro-American musicians — Biography. I. Title.
ML385.L69 1978   780'.92'2 [B]   77-22215
ISBN 0-306-77523-9

Published by Da Capo Press, Inc.
A Subsidiary of Plenum Publishing Corporation
227 West 17th Street, New York, N.Y. 10011

INTRODUCTION

Penman Lovinggood published this modest report on black music during a time when glorification of the black man's art, music, and literature was in vogue on both sides of the Atlantic. Moreover, it was a period of unprecedented cultural, intellectual, and artistic activity among the black peoples themselves, particularly in the city of New York. So distinctive was the decade immediately following World War I that it became known as the Negro Renaissance, or the Harlem Renaissance, and those who engaged in the activity were regarded as representative of the "New Negro." It was an area of optimism, exuberant exploration and experimentation, self-assertion, infectious enthusiasm, and rediscovery of the past. Although dominated by writers and poets — among them, James Weldon Johnson, who inaugurated the movement in 1917 with his publication *Fifty Years and Other Poems,* and Alain Locke, the spiritual father of the movement, who published in 1925 a collection of essays, stories, and poems entitled *The New Negro* — the era witnessed also signal accomplishments in music, the fine arts, and the theater. Indeed, it was the achievement of black musicians that provided another label for the 1920s — the Jazz Age.

The present volume is significant in the history of American music for several reasons: it was the first survey of black music since the epochal publication in 1878 of James Monroe Trotter's *Music and Some Highly Musical People,* and there was not to be another study until 1934, the publication year of Maude Cuney Hare's *Negro Musicians and Their Music.* At a time when the attention of the public was focused on jazz, this study offered documentation of the activities of black musicians in the world of concerts, opera, and the theater. Moreover, Lovinggood proved himself to be a prophet of no mean gifts in selecting his subjects; with one exception, a musician who died at the age of twenty-one, they all made lasting contributions to the society in which they lived. To be sure, he did not have to gamble on Coleridge-Taylor, who was dead in 1921, the year this volume was published, and three or four others had received critical acclaim in an earlier decade. But for the most part, the author was assessing the talent and potential of relative unknowns — and he proved to be correct.

Lovinggood was a practicing musician, not a historian. Although his vignettes are charming, he frequently neglected to include the kind of factual data that would help to place his subjects in historical context. Such information is not easily accessible for black musicians, of course, for few were included in the standard music dictionaries and histories. By consulting the valuable files of the Schomburg Collection (of the New York Public Library), I have been able to find obituaries in the black press for some musicians, and by contacting relatives or friends of the deceased, I have obtained vital statistics for others. In some instances, it was difficult to determine an exact birth year if the information source gave only the age at death instead of the month and year of birth. Included in the following list are references to biographical studies, where such exist, for the benefit of those who are curious to know "whatever happened to ＿＿＿＿＿ ?"

1. Marian Anderson (1902—   ). Kosti Venanen, *Marian Anderson* (New York, 1941; reprint 1976). Marian Anderson, *My Lord, What a Morning* (New York, 1956).
2. Henry T. Burleigh (1866—1949). *Dictionary of American Biography* Supplement.
3. Melville Charlton (1880—1973).
4. Samuel Coleridge-Taylor (1875—1912). W. C. Berwick Sayers, *Samuel Coleridge-Taylor: Musician* (New York, 1915). William Torto-

lano, *Samuel Coleridge-Taylor; Anglo-Black Composer* (Metuchen, N.J., 1976).
5. Cleota Collins (1893–1976).
6. Will Marion Cook (1869–1944). *Dictionary of American Biography* Supplement.
7. Robert Nathaniel Dett (1882–1943). Vivian Flagg McBrier, *R. Nathaniel Dett: His Life and Works* (Washington, D.C., 1976).
8. Carl R. Diton (1866–1962).
9. Joseph Douglass (1869–1935).
10. E. Azalia Hackley (1867–1922). M. Marguerite Davenport, *Azalia: The Life of Madame E. Azalia Hackley* (Boston, 1947).
11. Helen E. Hagan (1893–1964).
12. Roland Hayes (1887–1977). McKinley Helm, *Angel Mo' and Her Son, Roland Hayes* (Boston, 1942).
13. Kemper Harreld (1885–1971).
14. J. Rosamond Johnson (1873–1954).
15. R. Augustus Lawson (1875–1959).
16. Eugene Mars Martin (c. 1905–1926).
17. William H. Richardson (1869–193?).
18. Florence Cole Talbot (c. 1890–1961).
19. Clarence Cameron White (1880–1960).

EILEEN SOUTHERN
Harvard University

Famous Modern Negro Musicians

By
PENMAN LOVINGGOOD

Published by

PRESS FORUM CO.   **BROOKLYN, N. Y.**

PENMAN LOVINGGOOD

Famous Modern Negro Musicians

BY

PENMAN LOVINGOOD

BROOKLYN - NEW YORK
PRESS FORUM COMPANY
1921

Press Forum Company
Brooklyn - N. Y.

FOREWORD

A VOLUME of this kind must of necessity be limited in it's inclusion. It does not claim to be universal in consideration, nor all-inclusive.

That the Negro Musician has reached a point at which he needs to be chronicled needs hardly to be contended, since the trend of the moment, both professionally, and other-wise, is to give him further recognition, where further recognition is due. On the other-hand that the younger Artist does not receive more encouragement might be traced, to some extent to the fact that the sentiment toward the older Artist and Musician has not been sufficiently crystalized.

A book of eulogy it is, never-the-less, one of fact, with the ultimate racial evolution in Art as the foremost consideration.

Again we say, that, no claim is made to exhaustive biographical note, nor universal consideration. We merely set forth, that those here included are famous, and likewise Modern Musicians.

P. L.

SAMUEL COLERIDGE-TAYLOR

This Crowning musical genius was born in London in 1875 of Anglo-African parentage. His father was a medical student in London, and an under-study of one of the leading physicians of that great Metropolis.

His mother was an Englishwoman of fine taste and developement. Notwithstanding the objections of the family and friends she persisted in her regard for the native doctor and married him.

When Samuel Coleridge-Taylor was five years of age, he was discovered, by Col. Herbert A. Walters in a facinating game of marbles, with a small sized violin under his arm. This so impressed Col. Walters that he decided to investigate the home-life of this interesting lad. This he did; and after a consultation with his mother, he decided that the lad should be given a musical training. Thru the influence, of Col. Walters, he became a student at the Royal College of Music, where he studied violin, piano-forte, and composition. His Professor, at the Royal College, in composition was Sir Charles Villiers Stanford.

He began composing from the very start of his

Royal College experience; and before he had left College he had attracted the serious attention of the musical world, by the quality of his work in composition.

His first success was the Ballad in A Minor, for Orchestra. This work was composed, at the request of the Committee, of the Three Choir's Festival, thru the influence of Sir Edward Elgar; who had been requested to write something for the Festival, but on account, of other work, in which he was then engaged it was impracticable for him to comply with the request. He at once suggested Coleridge-Taylor. In suggesting Coleridge-Taylor, he characterized him, as "far and away the cleverest fellow going, among the younger men."

The commission also required, that the composer be present to conduct the the work at it's premier. This composition was received with such enthusiasm, and it was conducted so successfully, that a new, and greater value now rested upon all his subsequent works.

His next creation, "Hiawatha's Wedding Feast" was one such as to greatly broaden his claim to fame.

Difficulties of text appealed to him, as during his

Royal College days he had shown especial aptitude for strange words and rhythms. The presentation of this work was attended with such genuine approval that he was constrained to add to it "The Death of Minneha-ha," and "Hiawatha's Departure," and also an orchestral Overture. The Overture however did not become an integral part of the triology.

Following his natural ability for linking odd subjects to musical settings; he next brought out 'The Blind Girl of Castle Cuille,' and 'Meg Blane.' 'The Atonement' his chief essay into the field of oratorio is a fine work upon the subject of the Crucifixion.

A fortunate item in his whole career was the absence of the petty jealousies that are frequently indulged in by musicians. He had the distinguished co-operation of such men of standing as Sir Edward Elgar, Sir Hubert Parry, Sir Authur Sullivan, and Sir Charles Villiers Stanford.

In 1904 he made his first visit to America. He had for a long time corresponded with various representative people here, and he always expressed a desire to visit the United States. This wish was gratifed when in 1904 he was guest of the S. Coleridge-Taylor Choral Society in Washington, D. C. and conducted a presentation of "Hiawatha." He made in all three visits to America, the last of which was to conduct the "Wedding Feast" at a Choral Festival of the Litchfield County Choral Union, Norfolk ,Conneticut, at which festival Mme. Alma Gluck was Soprano Soloist, and he had the support of a full chorus, and a symphony orchestra from New York City.

Returning to England he was kept exceedingly busy in the role of adjudicator at many choir contests, and in the closing years of his career these duties were so numerous as to almost exhaust his physical powers. It was just after returning from a contest of this kind that he was stricken fatally.

Coleridge-Taylor's works comprise 83 opus numbers in the larger forms and numerous songs and smaller gems. He was a prolific writer and he burned his vital energy up in successive musical creations. His techique was inexhaustive and his dramatic propensities and musical perception were unerring. The Coleridge-Taylor harmonies are very strikingly individual, and even more so are the streams of inspiration which he pours upon his subjects and the subtle coincidence of the joining of the text and the music.

He stands immortally with the Masters; and is the greatest Negro Musician. Fired with the spirit of Mozart and the underlying rhythmic instinct of his native

race he carved for himself and for his race a place a-
mong the Masters of the Art. In statue he stands a-
breast men of modern laurels such as Edward Mac-
Dowell, Sir Edward Elgar, Edward Greig, and Moritz
Moskowski. He was pre-emently an individualist, and
for his own race the musical liberator.

He died in Croyden in 1912 of overwork, and
nervous debilitation; dying early as most men stirred
with the ambition for accomplishment and blessed with
a genius for creative work. The English nation mourn-
ed his passing as of one of her most worthy sons; but
in the hearts of the darker people's of the civilized
world the chord of sympathy resounded to the final
moments of this great man who felt the heart-pulse of
his race so nobly and also so thoroughly. Passing
at the age of thirty-seven; too young to die; he sum-
med up a life of strenuous activity and purposeful effort. A few hours before he died he raised foward on
his death-bed and in an imaginary concert hall before an
imaginary orchestra he conducted his last tone poem.

This man did more for the race musically than any
other, He set the pace far in advance of his time. He
wrote for posterity, and filled a void which had exist-
ed before his time. Like Beethoven his music lives.
He is, and will remain for us the one and only, the
first and foremost SAMUEL COLERIDGE-TAYLOR.

HENRY T. BURLEIGH

MR. HENRY T. BURLEIGH was born in Erie, Pennsylvania, and at an early age showed musical tendencies. Prominent Artists played, at home, for a wealthy music lover, of Erie, and, on one occasion he stood outside, in the snow, and listened, in rapt attention. When music was to be the order, of the day, upon subsequent occasions, he was permitted, to open the door for the guests, and in this manner he heard the best music, which meant so much to the impressionable lad.

In New York he entered the National Conservatory, which has been frequented, by so many persons of importance, in the growth of music in America. There he also ingratiated himself, into the good favor of persons, who could help him much. He did clerical work, such as addressing envelopes, and mailing cards, for Mrs. Mac Dowell, mother of Edward A. Mac-Dowell, and thus came into contact, with the guiding influence, and beloved parent, of another of America's great musicians.

His talents were many. He played tympany in the symphony orchestra, and became directly aquaint-

6

ed with the principal orchestral scores. He studied piano-forte, voice, theory, and composition. His baritone voice was such, that his major efforts were then directed toward his forth-coming career, as a baritone soloist, and even he, perhaps, was not fully aware, of the triumph, that awaited him, in the province of composer. He sang as if inspired; so thoroughly cultured so absorbingly musical, as he has always been, he sang his way, into the recognition, of public, musicians, press, royalty, and withal, held in reserve another side of himself, which was to reveal itself, and have him proclaimed America's greatest Art-Song writer, and the American Negro's foremost composer. We should not leave his career, as a singer, without remarking that, had Henry T. Burleigh never written a song he would still, far and away carry the highest honors of our musical compeers. In fact, so well is he known as a singer, that many very reluctantly relinquish this as the claim, for his highest honors. Mr. Burleigh takes this view himself, of long continued work, as a singer. Mr. J. Pierpont Morgan was exceedingly fond, of his singing, and the large congregation, at St. George's in New York, where Mr. Burleigh has been soloist for many years holds to him as a gem, too priceless to relinquish. Likewise, the people of the Temple Emmanuel of Fifth Avenue holds steadfastly, to Mr. Burleigh's services. King Edward, of England acclaimed him, and his own people clamour for his appearance. This experience as a singer would, alone, justify the claim to pre-eminence; but, when all the stories of his experience as a recitalist, and Concert Baritone are related, the twentieth part of the real Harry T. Burleigh has not been told. We have always held, that the creative genius transcends the interpretive artist, and a people who have no art creators have no hope of permanency in art. The genius in H T. Burleigh, not only moved him to this realization, but it gave scope to an inate dramatic propensity, that could not be lost, to the literature, of the race's musical treasure. Who is not arrested, by this peculiar dramatic trait, on hearing Mr. Burleigh's music? He has gone, from achievement to achievement. He started out with "Jean." The music world was struct, facinated, won, by this first venture of his. He called it just a little thing done between his exacting duties, as Church and Concert Singer. But the public saw more; something new; an element, that was more than just of the ballad type. It is best termed the 'Art-Song,' and Harry T. Burleigh has done much, to perfect this kind of song in America. Authoritive ones have admitted he is the foremost writer, of the Art-Song, and his subsequent resourcefulness has substantiated their superior judgement. After "Jean," has come Art-song, after Artsong. "In the Wood of Finvara," "The Grey Wolf," "Three Shadows," "The Saracen Songs," "Passionale," and many, many others. Mr. Burleigh is also on the Editorial Staff, of G. Ricordi and Co., of New York City, and puts in a strenuous day, in the copious rooms, of Ricordi.

The full stature of Henry T. Burleigh has not perhaps, been extended into the minds, of the people of some remote communities; altho he is known far and wide, his true worth will, perhaps, not be fully realized, until subsequent years have brought the added glow which accompanies the achievements, of the world's brightest, and most potent workers. Surely the work of this man has brought the music of the race more and more, into it's own. His work with the Negro Spiritual has been a devoted and masterful achievement, which has electrified the minds, of the music lovers of many races, to the full beauty of the music of this his own people.

The exceptional culture, of this man and musician has carried him into the most exclusive circles, and has won for him the respect, the honor, the love, and esteem, of the best people, of both races, in America, and of the people of prominence abroad.

Mr. Burleigh has a very engaging personality, is well-versed in subjects other than musical, and is an authority, on matters of musical import.

The style of H. T. Burleigh has become a thing of such unique charm, that one need only hear a few bars of a composition, to be transported, into the spirit of the truth of his work. The harmonic fabric of Mr. Burleigh's compositions are indeed revelations, and likewise, they are a forbidden measure to players unaquainted, with various structure of the unusual harmonic relationships. Mr. Burleigh has grown so steadily, as a composer, that to an increasing number his career, as a singer appears to have served mainly, as a stepping stone to larger achievement. He it was who was destined to perfect the Art-song form, in our midst, and to become pre-emenent in it's use.

In New York Mr. Burleigh is held to be the synosure of artistic epaulette, and will be found in exclusive circles. His worth is felt where ever the full value of art is appreciated. The English have a Cyril Scott; the Russian has Rachmaninoff; in France we hear of Leo Delibes. To America has been given the singular art of Henry Thacher Burleigh.

R. NATHANIEL DETT

MR. R. NATHANIEL DETT our most characteristically racial composer, who has ellicited much favorable comment and recognition, is a writer of unique attainments, and has had a varied experience, in the rise to his present position, in the Nation's music life.

He has risen steadily because of a large resource of talent, and again because of a decisive ability, to stick to certain lines and principles, which, as aforesaid, are distinctly racial; and he has won by these methods a-lone.

This well-known composer also arose from humble beginnings. Dr. John Ross Frampton, often, when referring, to the possibility of one's rising, from obscurity to great success, uses as an illustration Mr. Dett's singular rise to prominence. Mr. Dett first came before Dr. Frampton's notice, when he was in Niagra Falls, N.Y., in the capacity of elevator operator. Dr. Frampton's attention was called, by a number of his friends to the ability of a young coloured man, in Niagra Falls; and upon hearing him he was convinced, and it was decided that he should take courses at Oberlin.

When he had completed amplified courses, in the

special subjects, of theory, piano-forte, and composition, he went out to Chicago. Madam Hackley was brought into notice of his work, at this time, and her efforts were added to those of others of influence in behalf of the rising musician. He was appointed Musical Director at Hampton Institute, which post he holds at the time of the writing of this book, and his presence there is valued most highly, by both faculty and student body.

Mr. Dett has at various times captured a number of prizes; among these is a concert grand piano, and first honors for his piano-forte playing, in a competitive contest, by one of the large piano manufacturers of New York.

None of our composers has been busier with his favorite work. He has produced music, which has shown a progress, that it is encouraging to review.

Among the Choral numbers are "Listen to the Lambs," "O Holy Lord," "Music in the Mine," and many others. "Listen to the Lambs" is, in itself a masterpiece of part-song writing, and is rated with the most ambitious works of other than racial composers. His piano-forte music is as engaging, and portrays an intuitive instinct for the music of this instrument. Among these are included the "In the Bottom Suite"

which encludes "Night," "Honey," "The Bacarolle,"
and "Juba Dance." and the "Magnolia Suite," which
encludes "The place where the rain-bow ends," "Mammy,"and other beautiful pieces.   "Juba Dauce" is a
perfect specimen of the moving spirit of the Negro
Dance form, and sets forth the possibilities in this particular field. It is a most happy inspiration. Mr. Grainger
the eminent Pianist has adopted it for his recital programs and has made a phonographic record of it.

Mr. Dett's harmonies are indeed his very own, and
reveal the poetic vision of a true son of the Mother
race.   He has an abundant technical reserve and his
ideas are of an attractive order.

His success has come early in life, and much
clever work should yet come from his pen.

Mr. Dett has also given attention to the original melodies, and folk tunes, and numbers among his
arrangements such charming numbers as, I'm so glad'
'Paid my vow to the Lord' and other very fine settings.

He has as companion of his home, and his art the
former Miss Eloise Smith, formerly of the Martin-Smith
School of New York; herself a very fine pianiste, and
an accomplished Artist, and this Union now has the
joy of a young child to make the Dett circle complete.

Mr. Dett's work constitutes one of the most facinating chapters of our music writers. It is potent with
the very spirit of our people. He is unaffected, unas-
suming, and is the very essence of artistic finesse.

He numbers among his staunch friends such nota-
bles as Mr. Percy Grainger, Ex-President Taft, and
many others of prominence in our nation's varied life,
and activity.

He is one of the most well-known composers of
the race, for there is to be found in his music much
that is native to all, who are conversant with the native idiom, together with that individual strain that a-
wakens interest, and more than interest for the people
have learned to love these pieces.

Mr. Dett is a student of classic, and contemporary
literature, and from this source will doubtless subse-
quently come a larger offering in the classic form for
which' our music literature yet languishes.

Mr. Dett has done much to make of our music
the thing of beauty that it is to-day.

J. ROSAMOND JOHNSON

MR. JOHNSON is a composer, who has the capacity for writing very exceptional music, and is one of the famed brothers, who have contributed so much to our musical and literary life. These accomplished writers have won for themselves an enviable place in the intellectual and artistic life of the race. Mr. James Weldon Johnson is a Poet and Journalist of distinction.

Mr. Rosamond Johnson the composer is a wellspring of facinating melodies, and his insight into the weaving of harmonies, in which to encase these beautiful melodies is indeed illuminating. His moving style is always graceful, and the very heart-beat of a lover enters into the music of his songs.

In the golden days of the Negro Music Comedy, when our genius for the musical play was in the ascendency of it's brief-winged flight; when we experienced such dancing as Aida Walker did; then was the trying ground and the evolving period of such perrenially happy composers as Mr. Rosamond Johnson.

The team of Cole and Johnson was for many years one of the leading musical producing groupes in the States, and the efforts of these co-workers were given

the consideration, which was due such clever work in
the field of Opera Comeque.

Since Mr. Johnson has left the field of production
he has held responsible posts in other phases of the
music life of his people.   He was for many years the
head of the Music Settlement School, of New York
forstered by wealthy persons who are interested in the
race's musical welfare.   His most successful work in
composition has been done during this time.

Succeeding the numerous scores for the plays of
Cole and Johnson he has sent forth such delectable gems
as "I told my love to the roses," "Morning Noon and
Night," "Since you went away," "The Awakening,"
and "A Song of the Heart."   The song last named was
dedicated to Mr. David Bispham, who was Mr. Johnson's teacher of singing.

He has composed many Choral works among these
"O Southland" has received more recent favor.

This Composer has the native spark of his people's
love of the beautiful, and an individuality, which reveals the beautiful in ways that are distinctly original.

We all love the music of this delightful writer of
songs, which are true wine of our own vintage. They
are, it seems, spontaneous as the water in the valley
springs; and are refreshing as a drink at these founts

of transparent happiness. Turn from the measures of even the programed effective masters of the emotions who paint in heavy and vivid colours, upon the canvas of tonal effects; to the radiant measures of "I dreamt that you were a rose, that grew beside a lowly way," or "My heart is a golden Instrument," and know a-gain what it means to sing; to sing with an over-flow-ing joy, and the love of a pulling, throbing heart, that is to the life of one in love what the laws of Newton are to space. Folk would indeed fly off in ways, and ways, but the love of someone anchors us here, and we sing of our love, and we sing of our dreams, which are not welcome, if love comes not.

Some one once said to me : "how does he think of such beautiful music?" I would answer here : that he does not only think these beautiful strains into place. These are given to the elect by the Muse that gives thot to genius, and by love, which is the light of all Art, and love and the Muse go hand in hand 'till the work of the artist is done.

The art of the music writer is a subtle art. It deals with emotions, impressions, and those finer sent-iments that are in the very striking of a chord, and ex-pressed adequately, only by those writers who are a-tuned to the infinite qualities of a universally agreeable expression of musical content.

More than any other workers in idealistic material a musical composer is called upon to show the most subtle handling of his basic materials, and to effect a convincing work thru the medium of correlated sound, and chord constructions. Of course, in this task inspiration is paramount, as it has been proved again and again, that a commanding knowledge of the construction of chords, and theoretical ground-work is valueless without talent and inspiration.

Promethius secured from the mount of Olympus the brand that gave to mortals warmth and the power of successive ignitions, and passed it on to his forbears. This musical insiration is pregnant with the fire of true genius, which is the sum total of the numerous passing on and forward of the lighted torch of artistic faith, truth, and perception, to the best of the sons of the race which is ours. We have been fortunate in our many modes of musical and poetic offerings. Dunbar is ever best in his cheerful poems, and amusing dialect.

A joyful composer and a especially musical one is this ever charming, always tuneful, and inimitable J. Rosamond Johnson.

WILL MARIAN COOK

GENIUS like the recurrent seasons has many ways of showing itself. The subject of our present chapter is a genius, and this genius has given evidence of it-sslf in a number of ways. Born with an ability for playing the violin, he studied this instrument abroad, and mastered it's technic. Having more than the interpretive vision he mastered theory and form.

The career of this well-known musician has been varied and kleideoscopic in it's extent, and has brought to him honors, that bare testimony of the powers of the artist, and carry the stamp of true worth.

He is now best known by his compositions, aud as others have done he has turned to the folk spirit for the insentive for his work. "The Rain Song" is in the native strain. as is also "Swing Along," which is as good an example of this kind of song as we have enjoyed. "Exhortation" is a native sermon upon the advisbility of being cautious, also of being careful. It is a kind of composition that lingers with one. Such closely woven harmonies, as are found in the latter part of it. The parts linger on a plaintive, decidedly characteristic strain, that is unsurpassed in it's beauty. It serves beautifully to remind us, that our vast hope

of success lies in the fact that, we have a race con-
science, without which the whole fabric might be lost
in the sea of nonentity. Nations succeed very much as
individuals do, in which developement a distinct type
is necessary, and a working principle to fashion it's
course. In the larger sense we have developed a musical language of our own, that is of surpassing beauty.

Nothing has done more to awaken this conscious-
ness than the music of the Negro composers.

Again take that exquisite little song "Mammy."
Whose heart has not leaped up on hearing it played
or sung? It is the expression of the heart-throb of
a whole race in the fervent love of those who give
themselves in body and strength that we might be a
race.

The recent tour of the New York Syncopated
Orchestra, brought much favorable commendation.

Mr. Cook was revealed as a Conductor, in which
role he is much at ease. This organization toured the
the United States, and England and brought additional
laurels to it's Conductor, and it's founders.

In this composer we have personified the reality
of the cherished spirit of the Southern Cradle Songs.

Will Marian Cook has made the race literature
richer by his worthy contributions to the whole.

He was long associated with the Clef Club of New York, and is loved and honored by all the men of the New York musical organizations, as a man of large sympathy and fellowship toward the members of these respective organizations. His ability as a symphony orchestra player is equal to that of any Concertmeister in any of our symphony orchestras. It is this exhaustive ability and the great lack of opportunity that at times have made him pensive and misunderstood upon occasion. Surely he lives music! A more ideal rendition of Brahms' Hungarian dances I have never heard at any time, than his own orchestra succeeded in accomplishing under his vivid leadership. There are musicians, that seem to have a magic touch. Such an one was Paganini. Elements in the make-up of some individuals seem to be contageous, when the possessor chooses to use it, to hold a power of entrancing his hearers at will. This quality we find often in those who had an early aquaintance with the violin. Early Paganini was known to have posessed this quality.
Wieniawski was a seeming magician, and had a personality that thrilled, awed, and astonished. Ole Bull practically by force of a temperment alone thrilled three Continents, with simple melodies drawn from an uncanny instrument with strings, and a soul. Will Marian Cook's aquaintance with the instrument would

seem to explain his skill, in rhythm, nuance, and magnetic manouvering far from hackneyed ways. One forgets the structure, form, and style of the piece and is conscious only of delight in the pure, unalloyed movement.

So sensitive a nature could not help being seriously affected by the hardness of musician's lot, especially of one who held within him such talent as this man.

It is by his musical compositions that we know him best; but the almost tragic significance of the full account of it, and the part that seemingly causes most seriousness is the absence of media by which his great symphonic ability might be utilized, and the dearth of material by which his full measure as a leader might be taken. The Syncopated Orchestra was an agreeable entertainment, and worthy to receive laudation; but Will Marian Cook was looking far beyond the Syncopated Orchestra, when he raised his baton in the Acdemy of Music. He was looking into the faces of a hundred men; men of brown and of native hue, who were playing a symphony of a new World and a new race; with intimate strains from the old inter-woven, and the members of this orchestra were of the race of Will Marian Cook, while the actual players he had before him were just a few.

Thus goes the story of one of the race's greatest musicians. Tragic, facinating, truly inspired is the well beloved, and incomprable Will Marian Cook.

CARL R. DITON

MR. DITON one of our most virile composers is a native of Philadelphia, and a disciple of Mr. Constantine von Sternberg, and the Sternberg School of Music.

Mr. Diton early embarked as a player of the piano-forte, in which capacity he toured the Southern States, and the East. Realizing a hope of foreign study the good people of Philadelphia, thru the influence of Madam Hackley, came forth in benefit, and aided in the project of giving this promising musician European experience.

Mr. Diton's broader study was done in Germany a most fortunate fact, because it has imparted the firm ground-work of musical sincerity and solid worth and and has given one more real musician to be numbered among our artists. Mr. Diton shows his German training. His inclination is toward the weighty musical fare.

Mr. Diton is not over-fastitous, again one of his worthy qualities. Music embraces virility as well as the eternal feminine. In Germany the musicians are virile, which is, perhaps, what makes music there, the thing it ought to be, a part of the every-day life of the people of all classes.

This composer has taught in some of the larger
schools of our land, and has written music also.   His
compositions have come forth in agreeable succession.
While engaged in teaching in Texas he composed a
symphonic work, which shows an aptitude for work in
larger forms, and thru the press of the leading Music
Publisher we have received some work in smaller cast
that have been well received.   Among them an Organ
Fantasie on "Swing low Sweet Chariot," which work
was played at the Willow Grove Concerts, by Wasilli
Lepp's Symphony Ochestra, at which time Mr. Diton
was present and in the audience.

A Choral arrangement of "Deep River " has atract-
ed much notice.

Mr. Diton is Organist of the Saint Thomas Church
of Philadelphia, and divides his his time between the
music of the Church, composing and teaching.

In the music life of Philadelphia Mr. Dition occu-
pies a place of pivotal prominence, as also in the National Association of Negro Musicians his spirit of reserve, and thorough-going method is one of the salient
parts of this promising movement.

The type of musician that we have in Mr. Diton
is valuable in the Art any nation.   Among the Amer-
ian Negro musical adherents such work gives a tonic

effect, in the manner of revitalizing the race's musical stamina, and giving that added sturdy element, without which music of any groupe will grow more or less insipid. Many of the offerings of the current French School are distasteful, by reason of insipid manner of treatment, and a drifting toward luke-warm femininity, with the lack of a virile quality, which would be a savor in the tuneful porage. Mr. Diton's personality, and Mr. Diton's music conform to this sterile quality, that is likewise very evident in the race to which he went to learn the art of music. No trace of caddishness is evident in the work of this early disciple of C. v. Sternberg. The land of Listz and Hayden, Beethoven and Brahms breathes masculinity. The weaker sex in fact has had little to do with the developement of music in the homeland of the Masters. Women first achieved recognition in composition in France, and the works of Chaminade, and De Hardelot are beauties of rariest quality ; in Germany music is a man's art. Organists, Choir-Masters, Orchestral players, and Composers are men. The women inspire and are the audience. The great Wagner's many loves were always the occasions for his most inspired work. We are thankful that the women of Germany gave way to motives of inspiration, and the patroness role, as also we are glad that France gave birth to Chaminade and De Hardelot.

Mr. Diton has passed thru the plain of experience, and has seen the vital flow of his people's life and art. For this work he has prepared himself well, and creative effort reveals more and more the pure gold of the native musical mine, and well-spring.

The compositions of Carl Diton have gone into the catalogues of the leading Publishing houses. They are sane, well-conceived ,and would seem to promise a kind of music-writing that we will welcome as a strong pillar to our solid structure. In his work we may find some promise of a meditative writer, as a Brahms among us, whose harmonies appear like a copious plush hanging, and a rich tapestry; weighty, but beautiful; copious, but of harmonic sweetness. Such an one we have indeed hoped to see in vanguard of our Music writers. A promise of the fruition of this hope some are indeed hopeful to behold in the Philadelphia Organist and composer of the "Deep River Fantasie " Carl Rossini Diton.

recitalist of his race.

The actual worth of Mr. Hayes' performance is to be found in his complete devotion to the perfecting of his work, and his untiring effort, in making his programs interesting. In this particular there are none to excel him. These qualities added to the natural timbre of his voice, and breadth of his training makes him an artist of superior attainments.

The singular qualities of racial appeal have been meaningly kept in his voice, and a strong element in his successful appeal is directly traceable to these qualities.

In the singing of mezzo de voce passages his voice is of singular beauty, as it is again in cantilina, and he has the forceful utterance necessary for more dramatic phrases. Voices we have heard, which were perhaps brighter, and some as pleasing in certain types of songs but for a voice that fits into it's own peculiar style and that pleases in it's own peculiar way there are none that out-distance the tenor Roland Hayes.

This exceptional tenor has won wide recognition. His position today is practically what an artist would desire. He has made money and he has made hosts of friends.

He thrills with the fire of his love for eloquent art works, and is always his very in the songs of his

ROLAND W. HAYES

BORN in Georgia; educated at Fisk, it was as a
member of the Fisk University Jubilee Singers, that
Roland Hayes first attracted attention as a singer. He
was heard, by a wealthy enthusiast of Boston's music
loving groupe, who decreed, that he should have further musical training. This further training he received from the distinguished teacher of singing, Mr.
Arthur J. Hubbard tutor of many successful singers.

Mr. Hayes has worked hard, and gone far, in the
Art of Song Interpretation, and in the demonstration of
what can be done when one has a passion for accomplishment, and a desire for attaining the summit of the
professional high-water mark.

The Race has rejoiced, that in the evolution of
this singer there was a patron of means to make a
way for exhaustive training and proper presentation.
His earliest presentation as recitalist was in Symphony
Hall, Boston before distinguished critics and public, in
which environe he has frequently demonstrated his art
on subsequent occasions.

The rise of Roland Hayes has extended over a
comparatively short term of years, during which he
has risen steadily to the present position of foremost

praiseworthy things. While in England he was presented with a diamond ring, by the King and the Queen
for whom he sang.

His success proves the power of presistance, of
faith, and vision, and points the way to greater a-
chievement.

He embraces all the elements of the successful
Concert Singer, and has received favorable criticism on
both sides of the Atlantic.

Like all successful Artists, Mr. Hayes works hard
and long at a time, and amazes those, who happen to
know of the length of his very strenuous and long
engagements.

The American Nation is proud of the achievement
of Roland Hayes. Prominent mention is given him in
the leading Music Journals, and the Daily Press of all
fair-minded American Communities.

He arose to a position of power, and usefulness
by his untireing devotion to Song, and by his unfal-
tering attention to business.

All Hail! the well - known tenor, and the succeeding years should yet reward Mr. Hayes with further
laurels for his excellent work in Song interpretation.

native race.   Much that he has done is classed in the same category as the work of the best concert makers in America.

The last fifteen years has seen the growth of a concert system in America, that is vast in extent of territorial expanse.   Mr.   Hayes by a judicious system and ready adaptibility, as well as a good management has compared favorably with the most successful concert artists.   He is hailed as his race's greatest singer. Indeed, his work is of a finished smoothness, and a healthy quality that recommends him well for these signal honors.

The vast amount of work that he has done, and the incomprable manner in which he has accomplished it is in itself a feat of great magnitude.

When we first heard Mr. Hayes he was singing an exceedingly fine bel canto.   It was singlar in it's beauty.   He has gone thru transition after transition of variety in interpretive manner, but has ever held the singular charm, that is in itself the soul of Roland Hayes.

He has recently appeared in England with admirable success, the plan of this European tour includes other parts of the old world, and Africa.

It is within Mr. Hayes' province to do many

FLORENCE COLE-TALBOT

Florence Cole-Talbot is our foremost coloratature Soprano. Mme. Talbot has had a colorful, and interesting
career in the Music World. She has toured with one
of the Jubilee Troupes, that went out from Chicago,
and has more recently come into her own province as
Soprano Soloist.

Mme. Talbot's exceptional training was received
at the Chicago Musical College, where she was awarded a Gold Medal, for most excellent vocal work, and
the honor of appearing, with the Chicago Symphony
Orchestra, as Soloist.

Mme. Talbot's career has been an exemplification
of the truth that experience is truly the best teacher,
and her subsequent triumphs have proven again the
value of application tempered with head, and heart in
overcoming difficulties.

She has appeared before vast audiences of both
races, and has held a true standard of excellence thru-
out.

Her programs are composed of the best music,
and what is best in vocal art. Her vocal culture is
the result of long training, and she portrays the skill
of art in singing.

This Artist brings to her work also, a broad resource of individual talent.

Many trans-continental tours, and successive appearances have made this diva's name a household word on this Continent.

Mme. Talbot's especial work lies in the realm of the coloratura, and in the essentially lyric styles. She is supreme in this kind of song, and in her own way she presents them with naive effect, and charming success.

She views her calling, with seriousness, and has in her career, contributed much to the elevation of our recital courses.

The demand for Mme. Talbot's services is such that her engagements follow each other in rapid succession.

We have heard her at numerous times, and in various places, and always she is gloriously herself, and constantly brings forth more that is excellent.

In culture, beauty of expression, and a winning personality Mme. Talbot is one of the most engaging figures upon our Concert platform today.

As a patron of what is new in the Art this Singer has gone into the new literature, and other sources, and has given programs, that interest music-lovers everywhere.

The progress of her work has commended her equally with the beauty of her singing, and the superior manner, in which she has held forth, from season to season.

A truly great Artist we are pleased to behold in Mme. Talbot, and the praise that will ultimately adhere to her very successful career will be, not alone for the beauty of her singing organ, but as well for a superior mentality, which combines the new and the beautiful, with the old, revered, and classic; and for a culture, that sees more in Art than mere sentiment.

Toward a broader culture Mme. Talbot has labored, and her own career has been an exemplification of normal growth along these lines.

To Spain it's Patti; to Afro-America it's Florence Cole-Talbot.

CLEOTA J. COLLINS

Cleota J. Collins is the foremost Dramatic Soprano of her race, a race of lyric singers.

In the classification of lyric and dramatic singers opinions always differ. Some classify according to the tembre of the vocal organ, without really considering natural tendencies, temperament, and training. A more trustworthy way has been the one determining what style of songs one gets into best; that is gets underneath the surface of the song, for adequate, and in fact really superior interpretation of the song. Is it in the romantic song of the lyric style, in which the beautiful pearl of sentiment is revealed? Is it in the tense climax of a dramatic scena where tense feeling of suspence, and fervor of action holds one gripped in it's moving power? Most successful Concert Singers sing both kinds of songs, but by reverting to our original consideration, of what style of songs fit our singer best we are able to determine whether we have in consideration a lyric or dramatic singer.

Miss Collins sings dramatically, by both temperament, and training. Her contact with Mme. Lila Robeson of the Metropolitan Opera Company has awakened the spirit of Music Drama in her which naturally would seem to have been in existence before. The ability to sense a climax, and the almost enherent instinct to look for one is an unswerving indication of the true dramatic temperment. It is more than lyric diction that holds her audiences charmed It is a bit of insight into the situation, that prompted the wedding of the music and the poem that gives to her the power of control.

Those who have heard Rosa Raisa know that in many ways she is the greatest Soprano of all time. Those who hear Cleota Collins will know that this spirit unites to make Miss Collins the greatest dramatic Soprano of her race.

Cleota Collins was born in Cleveland, Ohio. Her father the late Reverend Ira A. Collins was a minister of high intellectual attainments. Her mother Mrs. Lucy A. Collins was a very cultured woman of great beauty, with a love of elocution.

Her singing voice was discovered by her father. He was one day attracted by someone singing in the yard outside the Church. From the window he saw Cleota bowing to an imaginary audience and returning again and again in response to imaginary encores.

She began her musical career in the Church Choir. She studied at Ohio State University, taking courses in

Public School Music, Theory, Appreciation, and the History of Music.

She has taught Music in the South, at Florida Baptist College, and at Samuel Huston College. Austin, Texas.

She was, never-the-less, ambitious for achievement. Her voice even then was a gem of purest ray serene. Experience, and further training, in hands of the Masters was the imediate goal of her dauntless efforts.

Two wealthy ladies, friends of music, and admirers of the fortitude of the courageous young woman now came foward and aided her in the obtaining of her life's dream. Mrs. Harvey Goulder, and Mrs. S. E. Ferris were benefactors. Miss Collins with becoming gratitude has always proclaimed, that she owes her success to the generosity, and kindness of Mrs. Goulder, and Mrs. Ferris.

Her entrance into the New York music life was an early triumph in her career. She was introduced as a full-fledged Artist, and she wore this toga so incomparably, that she was in a short time recogized as one the race's leading Singers.

This Singer has a personality. She is a personality among personalities. One to whom success would come in most any line of endeavor.

Her very considerable achievement has occured in a brief period of five or six years, to this the time of her wide popularity. During this glorious period of her career she has listened to the promptings of a sure guiding intelligence, and faith of her advisors, who saw possibilities above her own cherished hopes, and the probability of her present acheivement.

The demand for her has become such that her seasons are filled with engagements in advance.

Miss Collins is also on the Editorial Staff of our most beautiful and instructive Art Journal "Music and Poetry."

In Miss Collins we have a true Singer of the new-er order. The work of this Artist goes far toward the establishing of the new Negro in clearer light of thorough-going critical judgement.

MARIAN ANDERSON

Miss Marion Anderson, the Contralto is the youngest Singer of first rank among us. She is one of the most phenomenal, both in the rapidity of ascent, and in the excellence of her perfomance.

She is a native of Philadelphia, and is loved by the Philadelphians so that it is more than home to her but beloved guardian and patron city as well.

A bit of analysis will enter into our consideration of Miss Anderson.

In the investigation of voices of singers science has revealed, that amplitude of emission is dependent upon a relative amplitude of the vocal organ. After an investigation of some two thousand throats of singers it has been recorded that Enrico Caruso had the most ample, and the most perfect throat yet brought under investigation. Thus artistic judgement is verified by scientific research.

Without the aid of science at hand we readily venture the assertion that Miss Anderson posesses the most perfect vocal organ in itself in the race.

To add to this exceptional organ Miss Anderson has fine musical ability. Mrs. Agnes Riefsnyder her teacher, in Philadelphia, is herself a wonderful Contralto, and she has given Miss Anderson a broad knowledge of it's use.

She gives forth a prodigality of voice and tone that is unmatched in it's warmth. For a time she was so continually filling engagements that it was necessary to commandeer her time for the best interests of her work, and her career.

Her musical career began when she was a Sunday School girl in the Union Baptist Church. Her voice attracted the attention of the musical people, and she was given an opportunity to develope her unusual talents.

The vogue surrounding this Contralto's work and following began here in the East principally, and has extended thru-out the music centers of the Nation. No singer is more lauded than she. The principal part of her singing has been to her own people, and they have thoroughly appreciated her.

She sings in various styles, and has a strong dramatic tendency. One might crave the opportunity of hearing her in music drama.

In accord with her brilliant record we are ready to acclaim Miss Anderson in other parts. We have heard her sing the "Messiah," which is admirably suited to her, and in smaller pieces she forms a contact with her hearers that is hypnotic in nature.

She started out with pieces of the ballad type, and the short songs, which she did with great credit; the great ease and control charming all who heard. She has added the operatic aria, and the classic art song, and her growth has been full and normal. Full maturity has added polish to the pure gold of her youthful voice.

Her public has praised and has sung her triumph, and ardently comes to her praise again. Her hold upon all lovers of the Art will be continually intensified by the talent and art which is hers.

A truly great Contralto we see in Miss Anderson, and one of whom America needs justly to be proud.

WILLIAM H. RICHARDSON

Mr. William H. Richardson the baritone is a musician, who has seen much of the musical taste and life of our people. In capacity of Recitalist he has aided in the movement toward better music. In joint work with Mme. Maud Cuney Hare, he has presented the folk song, the classic, and the modern art songs in their best light and form.

Mr. Richardson received his training in Boston, center of music and musicians, his particular art is directly traceable to this training received in Boston. The music culture of Boston, though not the exuberant, and super-abundant quality of some Eastern communities, is never-the-less of a kind that well warrants it's renown as a center of culture.

Mr. Richardson is essentially a recital singer. He fits into the recital program, and his work will be remembered for this particularly.

We have heard him at many times, and in various places and his singing always gives the impression of one who is seriously engaged in the perfecting of true artistic interpretations.

Like many others of our singers, Mr. Richardson has traverst the musical centers of the nation, and has appeared before the select and elect, and the rank and file of our music-loving populace.

Mr. Richardson's is a manly voice, which portrays all the qualities that come from manly efforts.   He also sings songs of a delicate texture, which are no less pleasing.   The pathos of Negro music demands peculiar vocal nuance, and Mr. Richardson posesses the characteristics for singing the songs of his own people.

Mrs. Hare in lecture programs lays emphasis on the peculiarities of different kinds of native music, and Mr. Richardson illustrates that which pertains to song.

The importance of the lecture program cannot be too highly regarded, especially in hands of such competent Artists.   This kind of entertainment should become yet more and more popular, as a part of the actual education of the young people, and edification of the older ones.   They are sources of inspiration that lead to later day results.   They are sources of education that lead to further introspection.   They are refreshing when properly done.

Mr. Richardson has stood the test of long concert work, and has in midst of these exacting requirements purified the flow of his highly agreeable tone, and has amplified to full measure his tonal resourses.   The baritone voice quite contrary to the general opinion is a difficult voice to sing masterfully, because the great warmth and breadth of tone that is required.   One needs only to hear Titta Ruffo, or Straciarri to be convinced of this fact.   Mr. Richardson's is nothing short of the standard renditions of these Artists.

Musicians of Boston hail this Baritone and his accompanist heartily, when they come forth in recital preparitory to their going on tour.

The Nation has acclaimed this baritone, and his career is sybolic of the modern musician's attitude to his Art and to his calling.

JOSEPH H. DOUGLASS

Mr. Douglass was the first violinist, of our own Afro-American groupe to tour this Country, and gain recognition, as a violinist of national fame. He is the grandson of Frederick Douglass, and bears a striking resemblance of the famous Orator, and Statesman.

Mr. Douglass came upon the stage, when our field of Art was still a virgin one. He early brought talents with him, that were a credit to him as a musician. His playing revealed the touch of the real musician.

To audiences of the time of my own childhood, Joseph H. Douglass was an idol. He typified the upward strivings of a race in the field of violinistic art.

His playing was inspired. He united a brilliant technique, and a musicianship that was true. His programs combined excellence, with a kind of magnitism, which gives his hearers real satisfaction.

Mr. Douglass' playing carried with it a sense of poetry, and bordered on those fanciful regions, where dreams are made. His style was especially reminiscent of the works of Sarasate, and the fanciful School of violin playing. He carried his own temperamental a-tributes, and the under lying spirit of the music that he played, into an alliance, by which he profited.

He has held *a* very responsible teaching position in-cluding the Violin Department at Howard University.

This famous Violinist posesses an instrument of rare make and value. It was presented to him, at early age, by his Grandfather the Hon. Frederick Douglass, on this wonderful gift he has played his way into the hearts of his people, and to fame.

He is today one of our foremost musicians. The place he holds in the hearts of thousands of our music lovers will remain pre-eminently his own. He held a justly appreciated high standard of efficiency, in a field especially difficult, and in a manner quite unique by his quite temperamental, and graceful playing of the violin.

He very gracefully headed our own violin-playing groupe in America, making possible larger achievement. This gave to him an enviable place among our music-ians.

Mr. Douglass has recently taken charge of the Orchestra, of one of the new, and largest theatres in the District of Columbia, and the city of Washington. In securing Mr. Douglass the management has taken a long step foward in the obtaining of high class musical performances.

The theatre orchestra has, in a few years, become the medium for bringing the best music to the people. Our orchestras are in line, in this movement. Musicians of the kind that Mr. Douglass is, when placed in leadership of our orchestras will lend vitality to the movement, for better music, in connection with the theatres.

Mr. Douglass is today, in that after-glow of professional eminence, wherein the joy of the thing accomplished is vivified by the length of a brilliant serice. He stand today in the assurance of a life filled with import, bearing the proud distinction of being first Afro-American Violinist native born in the U. S. A. to obtain International distinction. Another signal honor is his bearing of the name, and being in direct line of descent from the father of his Race the illustrious Frederick Douglass.

CLARENCE WHITE

Clarence Cameron White, brilliant American Violinist, received his early training at Oberlin Conservatory of Music, which is in Ohio, and supplemented this with several years of training abroad. He was a pupil of the Russian Violinist, M. Zacherewitch, and a pupil in composition of the late S. Coleridge-Taylor.

During the comparatively short time that has elapsed since Mr. White's return from Enrope, he has attained, without any sensational advertising, and while still a young man, a notable place among American Artists.

Mr. White has attained eminence, not only thru the possession of the natural talents, that unquestionably are his, but as well because he has an unbounded capacity for hard work, and intelligence necessary to guide that work in the right direction.

Mr. White is also decidedly a musician. He has the tact for building interesting programs. In playing he unites an admirable technique, and a beautiful tone singular for it's breadth, fire, and delicacy of expression.

He puts into his concerts a continuity that makes them especially notable for this particularly.

He has a jovial personality, and bears the distinction of having, at his immediate command more witty sayings bearing upon the profession itself than any other musician we have the pleasure of knowing. This jovial personality has won him the distinction of being known thru-out the Country as "Smiling Clarence White."

Mr. White has attracted a wide notice by a number of compositions he has given to the press. In these he is naively interesting, and displays an ability for writing music of quite an attractive order.

In the past few seasons these violin compositions have been featured on the programs of the great violinists, such as Fritz Kreisler, Mayo Wadler, Zacherewitch, and others. During the season of 1920-1921 the "Bandana Sketches," were presented in Ochestral form, in Symphony Hall, Boston, under the leadership of M. Agide Jacchia.

He is yet considerably a young man and his creative work is well conceived, and mnch should yet follow.

In the musical and social circles of Boston, Mr. White holds justly a high place, and he has won the friendly regard and consideration of both the musical people of his own race, and of the white race also.

Mr. White has directed the Orchestra, and musical score of " The Open Door," a most excellent Pageant, depicting the literary, and educational developement of the race, which the Atlanta University has fostered and produced, in most of the large cities of the East. The musical numbers of this Pageant are among the principal contributors to it's success, and Mr. White's energy and ideas are vitally associated, with these successes.

The first Chicago Convention of Negro Musicians, which led to the establishment of the National Association, of Negro Musicians, was initiated and begun by the joint effort of the distinguished Violinist, and Professor Henry Grant, of Washington, D. C. In this movement, of which Professor Grant was first President Mr. White has had wide influence, and his efforts have been far-reaching.

Mr. White is recognized by the musical people of both races, as one of the race's greatest musicians. Surely none are broader in outlook, and technical resource. His musicianship is based on a knowledge of both piano-forte and violin, and his theoretical training was gained from S. Coleridge Taylor, which is the strongest possible commendation.

Mr. White is successful, because he also has business ability, and his various works are placed so that they receive the consideration due to them.

In Boston artistic circles Clarence Cameron White stands high, and in the regard of intellectual people all over our land.

Mrs. White is a fine accompaniste, and aids him often in this capacity.

The figure of this Violinist stands before us illuminated by the true light of musical sincerity.

Mr. White's work adds worth and color to our musical concourse, and violinistic arena.

KEMPER HARRELL

Kemper Harrell is head of the music department of Morehouse College, Atlanta, Georgia. He is also one of our leading violinists.

He studied in America, and then further amplified this by European experience.

Returning to his native land, he went into the concert field, with headquarters in the city of Chicago.

In his recitals thru-out the country Mr. Harrell has demonstrated the capacity, for unifying a fine technecal ability, with an art ideal that is convincing.

His performance shows devotion to art, and what constitutes the legitimate artist.

The instrument is his natural mode of musical expression. He goes about his work with an enthusiasm, that makes his efforts count much for the advancement of native talent, where it is found in super-abundance.

He has formed orchestras at Morehouse College., and has given performances of leading works, with prominent Soloists.

He is perhaps engaged in a work, that will yield fruit, of a kind, that will help to advance the musical taste, of the race. To take the genuine enthusiasm, into the provincial centers, and there to hold forth with ever renewed energy is by no means a small task, and such teachers, as Mr. Harrell deserve much credit, for their part, in this kind of work.

American music, like the music of other countries flourishes in the large cities first, and radiates to the provincial districts. But it does not flourish in full splendor, until reinforced by the provincies from whence come some of the most brilliant workers.

Atlanta is in some respects quite unique, though in the very heart of Georgia, it is a very bee-hive of Negro Schools, and Colleges. Atlanta University, Clark University, Morehouse College, Spellman Seminary, Morris Brown University are all situated in Atlanta.

Mr. Harrell in this of concourse of student life has advanced the musical appreciation, and interest in the community.

In this work of musical developement, his talent

as Director of Choruses is hardly less prominent, than his ability, with the instrument. In fact his fame, in this particular has spread with rapid strides. Combining choruses from various Schools, he has given performances that do credit to Atlanta, as a center of race culture, and reveal his prowess as a Director.

The field in which Mr. Harrell finds himself is a large and important one ; rich with undiscoved talent, and overflown with the real spirit of community welfare, and the real folk spirit.

In such environment has developed, and will continue to evolve much of the best that the race produces musically.

EUGENE MARS MARTIN

An Eminent Philosopher went thru the streets of an Ancient City crying: "Eureka! Eureka! I've found it! I've found it!". We say here of the subject of our present chapter, that at last a true genius for the Violin has been found among us.

The term genius has been used much, in these days of superlatives, and sepeculation has been rife as to the true significance of it. Some have called it an infinite capacity, for hard work. We use it here to signify an inherent insight into, and an ability for doing a certain kind of work exceptionally well.

Violinists are born, not alone developed, thru study and hard work.

Study the life of any of the great weilders of the bow, and those individuals, whose very lives are a happy adjustment to the instrument; in fact get behind their family life, and learn how not only they have wished to conquer the instrument, but that it has been an absorbing passion of their predesessors also.

It so happened in another case, that a very good
tenor in Bonn, Germany, could not reach above his
own shortlived heights; but his son, a Ludwig Van
Beethoven became the King of tone poets.

The violin technec of Eugene Martin should be a
source of inspiration to all, who know of him.   That
a lad of his age should play as he does makes us
hearten for the broad stretches of the future.

He has fire in abundance, which is constantly being
refined, and at each successive hearing his insight into
the art of the thing has grown, we find.

No greater proof can be brought forward, as to
the necessity, of parents thinking of their children
early, and guiding them successfully, than the effeci-
ent guidance of David Martin over his talented children.

This boy surmounts technecal difficulties, with an
exuberance, and apparent ease, that banishes the thot
of care.   The heart leaps up, when it beholds the fitt-
ing adaptibility of a young man for his instrument.

Here we have talent that will go into the depths
of the world's violin classics, and proclaim the ability of

the Negro, to interpret the Masters. Master-works were composed, for master performers, and we shall place our claim, with that of Hiefetz, Hubermann, Siedel, and Kriesler, we shall hear matchless themes brought forth, and our own race shall be givien the opportunity to say something in the language of the immortals themselves.

The Famous prodigies, of recent times, have fullfilled the artistic promises of their youth. They are to be found to-day among the leading torchbearers of the fire in-extinguishable.

This young man is to-day fullfilling his earlier artistic promises. In his work and developement the Violin portion of our groupe has made a step forward.

R. AUGUSTUS LAWSON

The instrument of Beethoven, Chopin, and Liszt has has not been neglected among us, especially at the hands of such a remarkable artist as Mr. R. Augustus Lawson.

Mr. Lawson is a product of that time honored Patroness of Art, and land-mark of Culture, Fisk University, of Nashville, Tennessee. He is far and away the greatest Pianist we have among us. He is rated with the best players of the Nation, and for clearness of style, and finish he is the peer of any player in the country.

His playing is Chopin-like in his delicate spinnings of melodic lines, and alertness to movements of tempo is a marked attribute to the success of his playing.

Mr. Lawson's playing is of that type that runs into the realm of true poetry, that transports one out of the thot of scales, appeggios, thirds, and octaves, and transplant him into an elevated state of being. The feeling of monotonous effort never enters into any part of his work.

He has been twice Soloist with the Hartfort Symphony Orchestra, and his successfnl renditions at these concerts have placed him in the front rank as an exponent of piano-forte music.

The Fisk University is justly proud of Mr. Lawson and his work, as his work adds copiously to the high standard of music there and his connection therewith renders her claim to fame doubly sure.

Mr. Lawson's art is not too frequently heard by his own people. However the position into which his talent has brought him makes it more than right that the utmost recognition should be accorded him.

He teaches in Hartford, and between teaching and concert appearances, in New England he finds time occasionally, to edify those of us, who happen to be in the storm-centre of musical happenings, and are looking foward to what is foremost in our music life.

The art that Mr. Augustus Lawson purveys is the pure gold of musical sincerity. When it is weighed with true understanding, it is found to be metal of a kind too infrequently found. We fain would hear Mr. Lawson's brilliant piano-forte playing more frequentlly.

The Violin has been termed the most difficult of instruments, and yet the piano-forte, with all it's multitudes of color effects, and intricate combinations of of harmonies would seem to be as difficult. Surely the piano-forte has a magic all it's own. The limpid chords of the deadened petal effects, and the crashing harmonies of the double forte take in a vast compass of feeling and color. Some of the most immortal of all musicians, as we mentioned before, such as Listz, Beethoven, Chopin, have risen to fame as masters of this instrument. Among the high lights in the musical firmament they shine most brilliantly.

Mr. Lawson our own fore-runner of our piano-forte virtuosi is highly endowed with the spirit that makes the masters live, and we hail him to-day our own giant of the key-board.

HELEN E. HAGAN

From the French School of piano-forte playing we have already welcomed an Artist that gives expression to the best tendencies of that great school.

Miss Helen E. Hagan is of New England origin, and studied at the Music School of Yale University, from whence she was awarded a Scholarship, for excellent work in completion of the alloted course, and the composition of a Concerto, with Orchestral accompaniment. So creditable was this composition, that it was the cause of wide comment in musical circles, and won for her the chance for study in France.

Her playing in Concert has verified the verdict of those, who awarded her the especial honors of her College days.

Miss Hagan continued her studies at the Paris Conservatoire, and she has imbibed the spirit of France in a way that makes her playing impressive for that particular reason.

There is an element of romance in her playing, and a certain play of the emotions, that brings one to the thot of fair France and her rose blooms.

During the recent World War Miss Hagan went faithfully to the service of a Country she had already learned to love, and showed devotion not alone to her own America, but to that fair land, where the Arts are pre-eminently alive.

Miss Hagan's position in our music life might be compared to that of the famous Maid of Orleans, who would not see defeat in her countrymen's strivings, and failings, and in Miss Helen Hagan we behold our own Jeanne D'Arc of the piano-forte keyboard.

Her playing reveals not merely a feminine temperament, but in her climaxes she transcends the merely feminine.

We have heard her in a performance of the Concerto, which won for her the prize at Yale. The impression was one of admiration.

Following the close of the War Miss Hagan took up her residence in Chicago, where she was hailed as a a distinct addition to the music life of that great City.

Her studio was in the exclusively artistic center.

This Pianist has the distinction of being the first pianist of colour to appear in Aeolian Hall, before the famous New York critics, and public. She appeared in a program of difficult works, that some of critics thot would tax the powers of the most veteran Artist. She made a most favorable impression on this occasion.

She has more recently married Dr. John Taylor Williams, of Morristown, New Jersey.

Thru-out the country Miss Hagan is known as an Artist of superior powers, and attainment.

MELVILLE CHARLTON

Mr. Charlton, our most famous Organist. is a resident of Brooklyn, New York.

His Academic training was received, at the College of the City of New York. His piano-forte training was received in New York also. He completed a course in Choir training under the famous Chorister of Grace Church, New York, Mr. J. M. Helfenstein and in competitive examinations he won a scholarship at the National Conservatory. His Organ instruction was received from Mr. Charles Hienroth. the Musical Director and Organ Recitalist, at Carnegie Hall, Pittsburg, Pa.

Mr. Charlton holds the degree of A. A. G. O., (Associate of the American Guild of Organists.)

In his present activities he is Organist of the Jewish Temple of New York.

Of Mr. Charlton's playing of Bach, the critics have written much favorable comment, and his recitals are composed of the best in classic and modern music.

Mr. Charlton's own composition, the " Poem Erotique " is beautifully inspired music, and it shows the hand of a real craftsman, in musical art-forms. This piece is not only in the classic style, but portrays much of color and interest developed along approved lines, which fact is very much in Mr. Charlton's favor, and indicates that he is a sane writer as well as an interesting one.

In the Ballroom of the Hotel Waldorf-Astoria of New York, Mr. Charlton has conducted Operatic per-formances, for the patrons. At these performances many noted singers were engaged   Mr. Charlton con-ducted, in a manner that evoked the approval of the New York critics, and added again to his large list of successes.   The Operas presented were " Ill Trovatore and " Martha, " with singers of Boston, and Chicago Operatic circles.

In an article on Organ playing Mr. Charlton has written his substantial idea,, to the effect that an Or-ganist must necessarily be a thorough musician. When one's musical equipment does not enclude a know-ledge Theory, Composition, and form, much is lost to any musician.

We of American origin are indeed proud of the achievement of Mr. Charlton. He has proven that one can be an American, and a Negro and become a necessity in the music life of an American community, unrestricted by the limitations of color or class distinction. He traversed a road direct to the first places in our land. These triumphs have not come easily. He has worked hard and long and has attained a high degree of efficiency. Perseverence has crowned his efforts, with success, and he is known far and wide not alone as the foremost Negro Organist, but as one of America's foremost musicians.

E. AZALIA HACKLEY

We have already mentioned, in connection with the careers of many of our best musicians, how that Madam Hackley has been a benefactor to them, in the role of patroness, and seeming fairy god-mother. A more unselfish Artist it will be hard to find anywhere.

Madam Hackley has given her whole career to the advancement of Negro Music, and to the discovery of Negro talent.

In the days of her concert singing, she was our most brilliant soprano, and she posessed an art that was filled with the spirit of the true bel-canto singing style. As a patroness of the Arts, and an organizer of Negro folk spirit, and as Director of Music Festivals Madam Hackley will long hold place, in our hearts and minds.

Madam Hackley has staged festivals, from East to West. With her illuminating personality. she has drawn forces together, from widely varying sources, and has played upon these forces in ways that are truly her own, bringing the Negro folk-song into a more engaging light, and raising it further in the hearts of the heirs of the creators of this beautiful music, as well as in the hearts of the white people of our country.

Madam Hackley belongs to that school of Artists in which Nordica, Melba, and Bernhardt are found. Dynamic personalities, with super-abundance of talents and strength to carry on.

When this Artist was a recitalist her lectures then fore-told the importance of her efforts in the field into which she has later carried her talents A woman of broad vision we think in writing of her of the career of the late Oscar Hammerstein. Like personalities of his type, Madam Hackley had visions, that are now being fulfilled.

To one, who has had the pleasure of hearing one of Madam Hackley's Festivals of native song, comes renewed faith in the possibilities of the race.

Those who know Madam Hackley personally give testimony of her constant devotion to her work, and superior energy in the accomplishment of it.

No History of the Music of the Negro will ever be complete, without an account of Madam Hackley.

Her efforts have done more for the race than any other, in the field of Folk-lore, and the Music Festival.